learn

sunrise sunset crochet afghan

LW1527

ochet ™

, fabric
Service

tents

free project sheet!

Introduction

BROCADE

JACQUARD

Slip stitch crochet is the oldest crochet technique in print. It was first referred to in 1812 as shepherd's knitting in *The Memoirs of a Highland Lady* by Elizabeth Groves to make warm utilitarian items such as caps, waistcoats and drawers of homespun wool. The earliest crochet patterns, published in *Penelop Magazine* in 1834, were for silk miser purses made with slip stitch.

Typically slip stitch crochet is worked through only 1 loop of the stitch in the row below. A stitch worked in the back loop (*see Fig. 1*) only looks very different than a stitch worked in the front loop (*see Fig. 2*), much like the difference between the look of a knit stitch and a purl stitch in knitting. Slip stitch in back loop only forms horizontal bars on face of the fabric, and the fabric lies flat. Slip stitch in front loop only forms verical bars on face and has a pronounced curl toward the face of the fabric.

Fig. 1
Back Loop

Fig. 2
Front Loop

Slip stitch crochet produces three distinctive styles of crochet—brocade, jacquard, and ribbing. Brocade patterns emphasize the differences in

look between working in the front loop only and back loop only to produce patterned fabrics. Jacquard patterns use one stitch throughout (*it can be either front loop only or back loop only*) but change color every few stitches to create a pattern. The 3rd use of slip stitch crochet is to produce a very stretchy ribbing. The ribbing resembles 1x1 knitted ribbing in both appearance and elasticity, the main difference being that slip stitch ribbing is worked at 90 degrees to knitted ribbing.

Slip stitch crochet can be worked in either rows or in the round. When working brocade or jacquard patterns in rows, the work is done in one direction only. The yarn is started and ended on each row. You may end up with a lot of yarn ends to work in if you don't want fringe. The reason that patterns are not worked back and forth in rows is that when you work slip stitch crochet back and forth a stretchy fabric is created which is how slip stitch ribbing is made.

Working in the round (*in a spiral*) allows you to work continuously in one direction without ends. You can work in the round as either a tube or a circle/oval. Tubes can be sealed at one end to make pouches or sealed at both ends to make a double-layered fabric.

When working in a tube the beginning of each round migrates ½ stitch each round so that the beginning of each round spirals across the face of the work. For the purposes of the patterns in this book, each new round is considered to begin directly above the beginning of the previous round disregarding the migration of the stitch. Just line up the start of each round above the previous start and disregard the ½ stitch. ∎

RIBBED

Pillow

SKILL LEVEL

■■■□
INTERMEDIATE

FINISHED SIZE

13 x 17 inches

MATERIALS

- Lion Brand Nature's Choice Organic Cotton medium (worsted) weight yarn (3 oz/103 yds/85g per ball): 3 balls #098 almond
- Size K/10½/6.5mm crochet hook or size needed to obtain gauge
- Sewing needle
- Sewing thread
- 14-inch square pillow form
- 1½-inch buttons: 3
- Stitch marker

4 MEDIUM

GAUGE

12 sl sts = 4 inches

PATTERN NOTES

Combines brocade for body of Pillow and ribbing for Flap.

The starting point will migrate right ½ stitch on each round for right-handers and ½ stitch to left for left-handers.

For the purposes of this pattern, each new round begins at the edge of the Pillow where it folds in half. Just line up the start of each round along fold.

Work in continuous rounds; do not join or turn rounds unless otherwise stated.

Mark first stitch of each round.

INSTRUCTIONS
PILLOW
BODY

Rnd 1: Ch 40, sl st in **back bar** (see Fig. 1) of first ch from hook, sl st in back bar of each ch across,

working in **front lps** (see Fig. 2 of Introduction, page 2) of ch, sl st in each ch across, working in rem lps of same ch, sl st in each ch around, **do not join** (see Pattern Notes).

Fig. 1
Back Bar of Chain

Rnds 2–51: Working in front lps, sl st in each st around, sl st in next st if needed to maintain edge (see Pattern Notes).

Row 52: Now working in rows, insert pillow form, fold top edge opening in half, working through both thicknesses in front lps, sl st in each st across, turn.

FLAP

Rows 1–13: Sk first st, sl st in each st across, turn.

Row 14: Sk first st, sl st in each of next 3 sts, ch 4 (buttonhole), sk next 4 sts, [sl st in each of next 4 sts, ch 4 (buttonhole), sk next 4 sts] twice, sl st in each st across, turn.

Row 15: Sk first st, sl st in each st and ch across, turn.

Rows 16–18: Sk first st, sl st in each st across, turn. At end of last row, fasten off.

Sew buttons in place on Body opposite buttonholes on Flap. ■

Lap Afghan

SKILL LEVEL

EASY

FINISHED SIZE
40 x 55 inches

MATERIALS
- TLC Essentials medium (worsted) weight yarn (6 oz/312 yds/170g per skein):
    7 skeins #2332 linen
- Size N/13/9mm crochet hook or size needed to obtain gauge
- Stitch marker

MEDIUM

GAUGE
12 sl sts = 4 inches

PATTERN NOTES
Item is worked left-handed; diagonals will flow in opposite direction for right-handed crocheters.

Afghan is doubled-layered, worked as a tube.

Work in continuous rounds; do not join or turn rounds unless otherwise stated.

Mark first stitch of each round.

INSTRUCTIONS
AFGHAN
Rnd 1: Ch 239, sl st in **back lp** (see Fig. 1 of Introduction, page 2) of first ch to form ring, working in back lps, sl st in each ch around, **do not join** (see Pattern Notes). (239 sl sts)

Rnd 2: [Sl st in back lp of each of next 10 sts, sl st in **front lps** (see Fig. 2 of Introduction, page 2) in each of next 10 sts] 11 times, sl st in back lp of each of next 10 sts, sl st in front lp of each of last 9 sts.

Next rows: Rep row 2 until piece measures 55 inches.

Last rnd: Sl st in back lp of each st around. Do not fasten off.

FINISHING
Fold tube in half, working through both thicknesses and in all lps, sl st in each st across. Fasten off.

Rep on opposite short end. ■

Brocade Hot Pad

SKILL LEVEL

EASY

FINISHED SIZE

6½ x 7 inches

MATERIALS

- Aunt Lydia's Double Strand crochet cotton (300 yds per ball):
  1 ball #443 victory red/mexicana
- Size E/4/3.5mm crochet hook or size needed to obtain gauge
- Stitch marker

GAUGE

15 sl sts = 2 inches; 10 sl st rows = 1 inch

PATTERN NOTES

Item is worked left-handed; checks will slant in opposite direction for right-handed crocheters.

Hot Pad is double-layered, worked as a tube.

The starting point will migrate ½ stitch to right on each round for right-handers and ½ stitch to left for left-handers.

Work in continuous rounds; do not join or turn rounds unless otherwise stated.

Mark first stitch of each round.

INSTRUCTIONS
HOT PAD

Rnd 1: Ch 51, sl st in **front lp** (*see Fig. 2 of Introduction, page 2*) of 2nd ch from hook and in each ch across, working in rem lps of same ch, sl st in each ch across, **do not join** (*see Pattern Notes*).

Rnds 2–9: [Sl st in front lps of each of next 5 sts, sl st in **back lps** (*see Fig. 1 of Introduction, page 2*) of each of next 5 sts] around. At end of last rnd, sl st in back lp of each of next 5 sts. You will now start rnds here.

Next rnds: [Rep rnds 2–9 consecutively] 8 times.

Last rnd: Fold Hot Pad in half, ch 10 (*hanging lp*), sl st in same sp, sl st in each ch around hanging lp, working through both thicknesses, sl st in each st across. Fasten off. ∎

Oval Rug

SKILL LEVEL

INTERMEDIATE

FINISHED SIZE
22 x 32 inches

MATERIALS
- Elmore-Pisgah Peaches & Crème medium (worsted) weight yarn (solids: 2½ oz/122 yds/71g; ombres: 2 oz/95 yds/57g per ball):
    5 balls #4 ecru
    4 balls #132 earthtone
- Sizes I/9/5.5mm and J/10/6mm crochet hooks or size needed to obtain gauge
- Stitch marker

GAUGE
14 sl sts = 4 inches

PATTERN NOTES
Use 2 strands of yarn held together unless otherwise stated.

When making chain-1 increases at ends of Rug, avoid stacking the increases directly on top of increases of previous round. Vary the placement of the increases to keep the ends oval by placing the chain stitches in the flattest part of the oval to round it out.

On outer rounds, if Rug becomes excessively wavy or cupped at ends, decrease or increase number of chains at each end. Blocking will relieve minor waviness or cupping.

Work in continuous rounds; do not join or turn rounds unless otherwise stated.

Mark first stitch of each round.

SPECIAL STITCH
Increase (inc): Ch 1 between sts as needed.

INSTRUCTIONS
RUG
Rnd 1: With 1 strand of each color held tog *(see Pattern Notes)* and size I hook, ch 31, sl st in **back bar** *(see Fig. 1, page 13)* of 2nd ch from hook and in back bar of each ch across, working in **back lps** *(see Fig. 1 of Introduction, page 2)* of same

continued on page 13

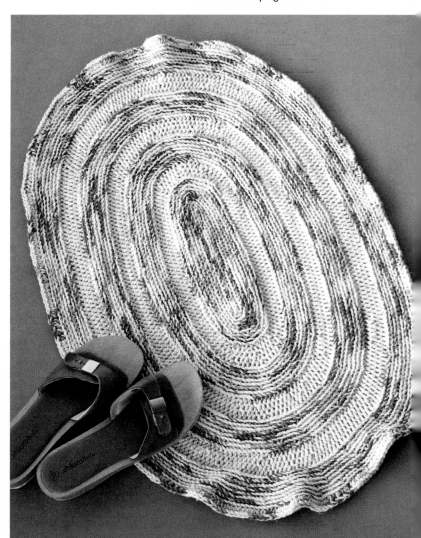

Jacquard
Hot Pad

SKILL LEVEL

INTERMEDIATE

FINISHED SIZE
6½ x 7 inches

MATERIALS
- Aunt Lydia's Fashion Crochet size 3 crochet cotton (150 yds per ball):
  1 ball each #6 scarlet and #423 maize
- Size E/4/3.5mm crochet hook or size needed to obtain gauge
- Stitch marker

GAUGE
8 sl sts = 1 inch; 15 sl st rows = 2 inch

PATTERN NOTES
Item is worked left-handed; stripes will slant in opposite direction for right-handed crocheters.

Hot Pad is double-layered, worked as a tube.

The starting point will migrate right ½ stitch on each round for right-handers and ½ stitch to left for left-handers.

For the purposes of this pattern; each new round begins at the edge of the Hot Pad where it folds in half. Just line up the start of each round along fold.

Work in continuous rounds; do not join or turn rounds unless otherwise stated.

Mark first stitch of each round.

INSTRUCTIONS
HOT PAD
Rnd 1: With scarlet, ch 51, working in **front lps** (*see Fig. 2 of Introduction, page 2*), sl st in 2nd ch from hook and in each ch across, working on opposite side of ch, sl st in each rem lp around, **do not join** (*see Pattern Notes*).

Rnds 2–16: Working in front lps, sl st in each st around, sl st in next st if needed to maintain edge (*see Pattern Notes*).

Rnds 17–34: Working in front lps, **changing colors** (*see Stitch Guide*) as follows: [change to maize, sl st in each of next 5 sts, change to scarlet in last st, sl st in each of next 5 sts] around, sl st in next st to maintain edge as needed. At end of last rnd, fasten off maize.

continued on page 14

Rib Stitch CAP

SKILL LEVEL

EASY

FINISHED SIZE

One size fits most adult women

MATERIALS

- Bernat Satin Sport light (light worsted)  **3** LIGHT
  weight yarn (2½ oz/182 yds/70g
  per ball):
    2 balls #04233 meadow
- Size H/8/5mm crochet hook or size
  needed to obtain gauge
- Stitch markers

GAUGE

16 sl sts = 4 inches; 32 rows = 4 inches

PATTERN NOTES

Looks and stretches like knit ribbing, but it's
  really crochet.

Cap is worked in rows running from top
  to bottom.

All slip stitches are worked in back loops only.

INSTRUCTIONS

CAP

Row 1: Ch 66, working in **back lps** (*see Pattern
Notes and Fig. 1 on Introduction, page 2*), sl st in
2nd ch from hook, sl st in each of next 4 chs,
leaving rem chs unworked, turn. (*5 sl sts*)

Row 2: Sl st in each st across, turn.

Row 3: Ch 1, sl st in each of first 5 sts, sl st in
each ch across, turn. (*65 sl sts*)

Row 4: Ch 1, sl st in each of first 50 sts, leaving
rem sts unworked, turn.

Row 5: Sl st in each st across, turn.

Row 6: Ch 1, sl st in each of first 50 sts, sl st
in each of next 5 sts on row 3, leaving rem sts
unworked, turn.

Row 7: Sl st in each st across, turn. Place
marker at beg of row now and each time row
7 is repeated.

Row 8: Ch 1, sl st in each of first 45 sts, leaving
rem sts unworked, turn.

Row 9: Sl st in each st across, turn.

Row 10: Ch 1, sl st in each of first 45 sts, sl st
in each of next 10 sts on 3rd row below, sl st
in each of last 10 sts on row 7 rows below,
turn. (*65 sts*)

Row 11: Ch 1, sl st in each of first 5 sts, leaving
rem sts unworked, turn.

continued on page 14

Winter
Mittens

SKILL LEVEL
■ ■ ■ ◻
INTERMEDIATE

FINISHED SIZE
Instructions given fit women's size 7; changes for sizes 8 and 9 are in [ ].

MATERIALS

- Bernat Satin Sport light (light worsted) weight yarn (solids: 3 oz/ 221 yds/85g per ball; ombres: 2½ oz/ 182 yds/70g per ball):
    - 2 balls #04233 meadow
    - 1 ball #03011 taupe
- Sizes H/8/5mm and I/9/5.5mm crochet hooks or size needed to obtain gauge
- Tapestry needle
- Stitch markers

GAUGE
Size I hook: 10 sl sts = 2 inches

PATTERN NOTES
The left and right mittens are identical.

The starting point will migrate right ½ stitch on each round for right-handers and ½ stitch to left for left-handers so that the beginning of each round spirals across the face of the work.

For the purposes of this pattern, each new round begins at the edge above the ribbing seam, and this seam is the outside edge of your hand along your pinkie finger. When ribbing is folded in half along the seam, the other fold is the inside edge of your hand along your thumb.

Work in continuous rounds; do not turn or join rounds unless otherwise stated.

Mark first stitch of each round.

INSTRUCTIONS
MITTEN
MAKE 2.
CUFF
Row 1: With size H hook and taupe, ch 15, sl st in **back lp** *(see Fig. 1 of Introduction, page 2)* of 2nd ch from hook and in back lp of each ch across, turn. *(14 sl sts)*

Rows 2–56 [2–58, 2–60]: Working in back lps, ch 1, sl st in each st across, turn.

Last row: Beg end should be on the diagonal from last st, join Cuff into a tube, folding Cuff in half, bringing row to front of the work and lining it up with last row, working through both thicknesses, insert hook through 2 lps on starting ch on opposite side of row 1, and in back lp of st on last row, complete sl st, sl st in each ch across. Fasten off.

Turn work inside out so seam will be on inside.

BODY
Rnd 1: With 2 strands meadow held tog and size I hook, working in **front lps** *(see Fig. 2 of Introduction, page 2)* unless otherwise stated, join with sl st in valley between ribs of Cuff at seam, sl st in each valley between ribs around, **do not join** *(see Pattern Notes). (28 [29, 30] sl sts)*

Rnd 2: Ch 1 *(mark as first st)*, sl st in each of first 14 [14, 15] sts, ch 1 *(mark ch-1)*, sl st in each of next 14 [15, 15] sts.

continued on page 15

Rib Stitch Scarf

SKILL LEVEL

EASY

FINISHED SIZE

4 x 33 inches, excluding fringe

MATERIALS

- Bernat Satin Sport light (light worsted) weight yarn (3 oz/221 yds/85g per ball):
  1 ball #3011 taupe
- Size I/9/5.5mm crochet hook or size needed to obtain gauge

GAUGE

16 sl sts = 3½ inches; 32 rows = 4 inches

PATTERN NOTE

Looks and stretches like knit ribbing, but it's really crochet.

INSTRUCTIONS

SCARF

Row 1: Ch 26, sl st in **back bar** (*see Fig. 1*) of 2nd ch from hook and in back bar of each st across, ch 176, turn.

Fig. 1
Back Bar of Chain

Row 2: Sl st in back bar of 2nd ch from hook and in back bar of each of next 24 chs, sl st in **back lp** (*see Fig. 1 of Introduction, page 2*) of each of next 150 chs across, ch 26, turn.

Rows 3–32: Sl st in back bar of 2nd ch from hook and in back bar of each ch across, sl st in back lp of each of next 150 sts, ch 26, turn.

Last row: Sl st in back bar of 2nd ch from hook and in back bar of each ch across, sl st in next st. Fasten off. ∎

Cabled Stripes Purse

SKILL LEVEL

INTERMEDIATE

FINISHED SIZE
4¹⁄₂ x 5 inches, excluding buttons and shoulder strap

MATERIALS
- Lion Brand Glitterspun medium (worsted) weight yarn (1¾ oz/ 115 yds/50g per ball):
    1 ball each #153 onyx and #170 gold
- Size G/6/4mm crochet hook or size needed to obtain gauge
- Tapestry needle
- 10mm wood beads: 3
- Stitch marker

GAUGE
26 sl sts = 4 inches

PATTERN NOTES
Technically, the beginning of each round migrates ½ stitch each round so that the beginning of each round spirals across the face of the work.

For the purposes of this pattern, each new round begins at the edge of the Purse where it folds in half. Just line up the start of each round along fold.

Work in continuous rounds; do not join or turn rounds unless otherwise stated.

Mark first stitch of each round.

INSTRUCTIONS
PURSE
BODY
Rnd 1: With onyx, ch 30, sl st in **back bar** (see Fig. 1) of first ch from hook and in back bar of each ch across, working in **back lps** (see Fig. 1 of Introduction, page 2), sl st in back lp of each ch across, working in **front lp** (see Fig. 2 of Introduction, page 2), sl st in front lp of each ch across, **do not join** (see Pattern Notes).

Fig. 1
Back Bar of Chain

Rnds 2–7: Working in back lps, sl st in each st around, sl st in next st if needed to maintain edge (see Pattern Notes).

Rnd 8: Drop onyx, **do not fasten off**, join gold in back lp of first st, sl st in back lp of each st around, maintaining beg st at edge.

Rnd 9: Work this rnd loosely, [sk first st, sl st in back lp of next st, sl st in back lp of st just skipped] around maintaining beg st at edge.

Rnd 10: Do not work in either of top lps of rnd 9, turn work with back facing, there is line of gold formed by 2 overlapping strands, sl st in each st of overlapping strands, maintaining beg st at edge, drop gold and pick up onyx.

Rnds 11–34: [Rep rnds 5–10 consecutively] 4 times.

Rnds 35–41: With onyx, sl st in back lp of each st around maintaining beg st at edge.

Rnd 42: Working in back lps, sl st in each st across first 30 sts (front), sl st in each of next 9 sts, [ch 5, working back across sts just worked, sk last 4 sts, sl st in next st *(button lp)*, sl st in back bar of each ch across, sl st in each of next 7 sts on Body] twice, ch 5, sk last 4 sts worked, sl st in next st, sl st in back bar of each ch across, sl st in each st around Body to last st, working in both lps, sl st in last st, this st should be at the edge. **Do not fasten off.**

SHOULDER STRAP
Ch 150, sk next 30 sts on Body, which should be at the opposite edge of Purse, sl st in both lps of next st, sl st in back bar of each ch across, sl st in both lps of next st on Purse. Fasten off.

BUTTON
MAKE 3.
Rnd 1: With gold, leaving 8-inch end, ch 8, sl st in first ch to form ring, working in back lps, sl st in each ch around, **do not join.**

Rnds 2–6: Working in back lps, sl st in each st around. At end of last rnd, leaving 8-inch end, fasten off.

Weave 8-inch end of last rnd through top of sts, pull to close, secure end.

FINISHING
Place 1 bead in Button, weave 8-inch end through bottom of starting ch, pull to close. Sew Button to top edge of Purse opposite 1 button lp.

Rep with rem Buttons. ∎

Oval Rug
continued from page 7

ch, sl st in back lp of each ch across to last ch, (ch 1, sl st) twice in last ch, working in **front lps** *(see Fig. 2 of Introduction, page 2)*, sl st in each ch across to last st, (ch 1, sl st) twice in last st, **do not join** *(see Pattern Notes).*

Fig. 1
Back Bar of Chain

Rnds 2–5: Working in back lps, sl st in each st around, evenly spacing 2 **inc** *(see Special Stitch)* around each end *(see Pattern Notes).*

Rnds 6–9: Working in back lps, sl st in each st around, evenly spacing 3 inc around each end. At end of last rnd, fasten off earthtone.

Rnd 10: Holding 2 strands of ecru tog, working in back lps, sl st in each st around, evenly spacing 3 inc around each end.

Rnds 11–14: With size J hook, working in front lps, sl st in each st around, evenly spacing 3 inc around each end. At end of last rnd, fasten off 1 strand of ecru.

Rnd 15: With 1 strand of each color held tog, working in front lps, sl st in each st around, evenly spacing 3 inc around each end.

Rnds 16–22: Working in back lps, sl st in each st around, evenly spacing 3 inc around each end. At end of last rnd, fasten off.

Rnds 23–48: [Rep rnds 10–22 consecutively] twice.

Rnd 49: Sc in each st around, **do not inc**, ending with sl st in back lp of beg sc, sl st in both lps of next st. Fasten off.

Wet thoroughly and block. ∎

Jacquard Hot Pad
continued from page 8

Rnds 35–51: With scarlet, working in front lps, sl st in each st around, sl st in next st if needed to maintain edge.

Row 52: Fold Pot Holder in half, ch 10, sl st in same st, sl st in **back bar** *(see Fig. 1)*

of each ch across, working through both thickness, sl st in each st around. Fasten off. ■

Fig. 1
Back Bar of Chain

Rib Stitch Cap
continued from page 9

Row 12: Sl st in each st across, turn.

Row 13: Ch 1, sl st in each of first 5 sts, sl st in each st across, turn. *(65 sl sts)*

Row 14: Ch 1, sl st in each of first 50 sts, leaving rem sts unworked, turn.

Row 15: Sl st in each st across, turn.

Row 16: Ch 1, sl st in each of first 50 sts, sl st in each of next 5 sts on 3 rows below, leaving rem sts unworked, turn.

Row 17: Sl st in each st across, turn. Place marker at beg of row now and each time row 17 is repeated

Row 18: Ch 1, sl st in each of first 45 sts, leaving rem sts unworked, turn.

Row 19: Sl st in each st across, turn.

Row 20: Ch 1, sl st in each of first 45 sts, sl st in each of next 10 sts 3 rows below, sl st in each of last 10 sts 7 rows below, turn. *(65 sts)*

Row 21: Ch 1, sl st in each of first 5 sts, leaving rem sts unworked, turn.

Next rows: [Rep rows 2–11 consecutively] 17 times.

Next rows: Rep rows 2 and 3.

Last row: Fold Cap and match row 1 and last row tog, working through both thicknesses, working through both lps on starting ch on opposite side of row 1 and in back lp of sts on last row, sl st in each st across. Fasten off.

Turn work inside out so seam will be on the inside.

TIE
Ch 65, sl st in **back bar** *(see Fig. 1)* of 2nd ch from hook and in back bar of each ch across. Fasten off.

Fig. 1
Back Bar of Chain

Weave Tie through rows at markers around top edge of Cap. Pull to close and tie in bow. ■

Winter Mittens

continued from page 10

Rnd 3: Sl st in front lp of first ch-1, *sl st in front lp of each st across** to ch-1, sl st in ch-1, ch 1 *(mark ch-1)*, rep from * around, ending last rep at **. *(35 [38, 40] sl sts)*

Rnds 4–8 [4–10, 4–11]: *Sl st in front lp of each st across** to ch-1, sl st in ch-1, ch 1 *(mark ch-1)*, rep from * around, ending last rep at **.

Rnd 9 [11, 12]: Sl st in each st and in each marked ch around. *(36 [39, 41] sl sts)*

Rnds 10–12 [12 & 13, 13 & 14]: Sl st in each st around.

Rnd 13 [14, 15]: Count back 4 [4, 5] sts on 1 side of inside edge directly above marker and mark, count back 4 [5, 5] sts on other side of inside edge and mark, sl st in front lp of each st to marked st, do not work in marked st, ch 5, sl st in front lp of st after next marker, sl st in each st around.

Rnd 14 [15, 16]: Sl st in each st and in back lp of each ch around.

Rnds 15–35 [16–36, 17–37] or to desired length: Sl st in each st around. Lengthen or shorten by working more or less rnds.

Rnd 36 [37, 38]: [**Sl st dec** *(see Stitch Guide)* in next 2 sts] around. If you have an extra st at end, sl st in last st.

Rnd 37 [38, 39]: Sl st in each st around.

Rnd 38 [39, 40]: Rep rnd 36 [37, 38]. Leaving long end, fasten off.

Weave long end through outside toward inside under front lp of each st around. Pull to close. Secure end.

THUMB

Rnd 1: With 2 strands of meadow and size I hook, working in ch-5 sps and sk sts on rnd 12 [13, 14], join with sl st in center ch of ch-5, sl st in each of next 2 chs, sl st dec in last ch worked in, in vertical strand and in front lp of first st, sl st in each of next 6 [7, 8] sts, sl st dec in last st and vertical strand, sl st in each of last 2 chs. *(13 [14, 15] sl sts)*

Rnd 2: Sl st in each st around.

Rnds 3–11: Sl st in each st around. Lengthen or shorten Thumb by working more or less rnds.

Rnd 12: [Sl st dec in next 2 sts] around, if you have an extra st at end, sl st in last st. Leaving long end, fasten off.

Weave long end from outside toward inside, under front lp of each st around. Pull to close. Secure end. ∎

TOLL-FREE ORDER LINE or to request a free catalog (800) LV-ANNIE (800) 582-6643
Customer Service (800) AT-ANNIE (800) 282-6643, **Fax** (800) 882-6643
Visit anniesattic.com

We have made every effort to ensure the accuracy and completeness of these instructions.
We cannot, however, be responsible for human error, typographical mistakes or variations in individual work.

ISBN: 978-1-59635-215-5

Stitch Guide

For more complete information, visit **FreePatterns.com**

ABBREVIATIONS

beg	begin/begins/beginning
bpdc	back post double crochet
bpsc	back post single crochet
bptr	back post treble crochet
CC	contrasting color
ch(s)	chain(s)
ch-	refers to chain or space previously made (i.e. ch-1 space)
ch sp(s)	chain space(s)
cl(s)	cluster(s)
cm	centimeter(s)
dc	double crochet (singular/plural)
dc dec	double crochet 2 or more stitches together, as indicated
dec	decrease/decreases/decreasing
dtr	double treble crochet
ext	extended
fpdc	front post double crochet
fpsc	front post single crochet
fptr	front post treble crochet
g	gram(s)
hdc	half double crochet
hdc dec	half double crochet 2 or more stitches together, as indicated
inc	increase/increases/increasing
lp(s)	loop(s)
MC	main color
mm	millimeter(s)
oz	ounce(s)
pc	popcorn(s)
rem	remain/remains/remaining
rep(s)	repeat(s)
rnd(s)	round(s)
RS	right side
sc	single crochet (singular/plural)
sc dec	single crochet 2 or more stitches together, as indicated
sk	skip/skipped/skipping
sl st(s)	slip stitch(es)
sp(s)	space(s)/spaced
st(s)	stitch(es)
tog	together
tr	treble crochet
trtr	triple treble
WS	wrong side
yd(s)	yard(s)
yo	yarn over

Chain—ch: Yo, pull through lp on hook.

Slip stitch—sl st: Insert hook in st, pull through both lps on hook.

Single crochet—sc: Insert hook in st, yo, pull through st, yo, pull through both lps on hook.

Front post stitch—fp: Back post stitch—bp: When working post st, insert hook from right to left around post st on previous row.

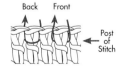

Front loop—front lp Back loop— back lp

Front Loop Back Loop

Half double crochet— hdc: Yo, insert hook in st, yo, pull through st, yo, pull through all 3 lps on hook.

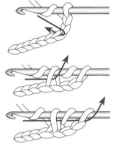

Double crochet—dc: Yo, insert hook in st, yo, pull through st, [yo, pull through 2 lps] twice.

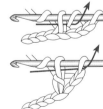

Change colors: Drop first color; with 2nd color, pull through last 2 lps of st.

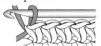

Treble crochet—tr: Yo twice, insert hook in st, yo, pull through st, [yo, pull through 2 lps] 3 times.

Double treble crochet—dtr: Yo 3 times, insert hook in st, yo, pull through st, [yo, pull through 2 lps] 4 times.

Single crochet decrease (sc dec): (Insert hook, yo, draw lp through) in each of the sts indicated, yo, draw through all lps on hook.

Example of 2-sc dec

Half double crochet decrease (hdc dec): (Yo, insert hook, yo, draw lp through) in each of the sts indicated, yo, draw through all lps on hook.

Example of 2-hdc dec

Double crochet decrease (dc dec): (Yo, insert hook, yo, draw loop through, draw through 2 lps on hook) in each of the sts indicated, yo, draw through all lps on hook.

Example of 2-dc dec

Example of 2-tr dec

Treble crochet decrease (tr dec): Holding back last lp of each st, tr in each of the sts indicated, yo, pull through all lps on hook.

US		UK
sl st (slip stitch)	=	sc (single crochet)
sc (single crochet)	=	dc (double crochet)
hdc (half double crochet)	=	htr (half treble crochet)
dc (double crochet)	=	tr (treble crochet)
tr (treble crochet)	=	dtr (double treble crochet)
dtr (double treble crochet)	=	ttr (triple treble crochet)
skip	=	miss